WIESBADEN

Jewel Box of Germany

By
Henry Guntrum
&
Freeman Wood

Published and printed by
Publications: Druckerei Chmielorz - 11 a Herrnmühlgasse - Wiesbaden, Germany

Contents

A pictorial documentary of the City of Wiesbaden in three parts:

Forword

In a most vivid and colorful way, this book offers an impressive view of the many beauties of our city as may be vouched for by the many visitors from throughout the world and by the American families who live here.

It is hoped that the pictures and stories of this publication will help not only to create a better understanding of the essence, history and problems of our city, but to gain new friends and to hold their friendship for many years to come.

The city of Wiesbaden wishes to extend a special invitation to all new visitors and hopes that all old friends will have the opportunity to return in later years.

Dr. ERICH MIX
Lord Mayor of Wiesbaden

Introduction

This book has been compiled to introduce the reader to what we consider one of the most beautiful cities in the world. It was designed to bring out the prominent points of interest to newcomers and to point out a few sidelights that may not be known to people who are already familiar with the city of Wiesbaden.

The facts and photographs have been checked with the most competent authorities to assure their authenticity. We could have written about many more interesting sites and scenes in and around Wiesbaden, however, we chose what we felt were the most outstanding.

We wish to give special thanks to the many city agencies which cooperated wholeheartedly with us in the publication of the book.

The Authors

History of Wiesbaden

The sparkling city of Wiesbaden, with its more than 250,000 inhabitants, is located in the Rhein River Valley in western Germany, some 25 miles from the major German city of Frankfurt and about 100 miles from the French border. Long known as a resort city, it is amazing to note that though it is nearly as far north as Hudson Bay in Canada, its climate is quite temperate. The summer weather is comparable to that of the northern United States and the winters are mild, much like those in Virginia and North Carolina.

Indeed, the winters in the Bavarian Alps, some 300 miles to the south, are far more severe than those in Wiesbaden. This may be explained largely by the natural hot springs under the city; the possible benefits of the Gulf Stream at the French and Belgium coasts; and the natural protection of the surrounding Taunus Mountains.

Arrival of the Franks around 500 AD

Wiesbaden's beginning lies in an obscure darkness. Historians have found stone-age relics that testify to a community life that existed in the pleasant valley between the Rhein River and the Taunus Mountains many thousands of years be-

Roman life in Wiesbaden during the middle of the third century

fore the Birth of Christ. Students of ancient geology believe that the area which is now Wiesbaden was once a vast swamp land.

The Romans are generally credited with draining the swamp lands to construct the city around the natural hot springs which were prevalent. Their advanced techniques were supposedly used to turn the wilderness into a stable foundation for the growing town. While a small farming community was probably established near the bogs, the advancing legions of the Roman Empire did a great deal to found the city.

Historians have found evidence that points to the invasion of Celtic tribes nearly 1,500 years before the Birth of Christ. Tombs and remnants of their civilization have been found in the nearby Taunus Mountains. The word Taunus is derived from the ancient Celtic meaning "protective barrier," taken from the natural protection offered by the mountains.

During the fourth century B. C., the Teutons (Germanic Tribes) waged a successful war against the Celts, ousting them from the country. Their victory was short lived, however, as the Romans advanced soon afterward and took complete control of the area.

After a 300-year reign by the Romans, the Teutonic Tribes began to rebuild and renewed their conflict with the invaders. The Teutons had gathered considerable strength, forcing the Romans to withdrawn and construct numerous fortifications — the Old Roman Wall of Wiesbaden is one of the few remaining structures resulting from these wars.

Eventually, the Romans, realizing the precariousness of their position, retreated to their castles and walled-in cities where they retained their security until the third century A. D. During that period, the Teutonic Tribes developed to such an extent that they were powerful enough to retake command of the countryside. Even the great Heathen Wall, built in Wiesbaden by the Romans, was not strong enough to suppress their advance.

During the period of their security in Wiesbaden, from 12 B. C. until the fourth century, the Romans enjoyed a very comfortable life within the city. They constructed several bathing installations — utilizing the natural hot springs — which were available to visiting dignitaries of commercial, political and military esteem.

During the middle of the third century, the Romans began to lose their power. The Teutons, coming from the southeastern portion of Europe, pushed the Romans slowly westward toward the Rhein. The fortress which

Wiesbaden in 1624. Copper plate engraving by Meissner

The Taunus Bahnhof in 1840

was built by the Romans on the highest point within the city was conquered and completely destroyed by the avenging Teutons during the later part of the third century. As a final effort, in 371 A. D., the Romans launched a counterattack, were victorious, and occupied the city for several more years.

From about 400 A. D., until the end of the fifth century, the history of the city is obscure. About 500 A. D., the land was invaded by the Franks. They conquered the country and levied high taxes upon the landowners. The Franks were responsible for changing the name of the city to Wisibada, meaning "meadow bath" from which the present-day name was derived. The Franks remained until the beginning of the Middle Ages and added to the walls and fortifications built by the earlier Romans.

During the fifteenth and sixteenth centuries, Wiesbaden again became famous because of the medicinal powers of its underground springs, the news of which soon spread throughout Europe and the Old World. The main hotels and inns of the city offered only a place of lodging and bathing facilities. A mutual agreement between the bath house owners and the restaurant owners sent the lodgers out for their meals.

Wiesbaden During the Middle Ages

During the Middle Ages, the country more or less leveled off into a monarchistic type of government, with the royalists reigning supreme. The Counts of Nassau became the rulers of the growing city of Wiesbaden and the surrounding countryside. They proved to be both good and bad, and statues of many of these rulers may be found within the city today.

The Counts of Nassau are responsible for the erection of many of the more famous buildings and sites now enjoyed by visitors to Wiesbaden. Local Wiesbadeners supplemented their income by conducting tours of the city and recommending the better restaurants.

In 1547 the city was destroyed by fire and only the royal castle and some ten houses remained.

Wiesbaden again suffered during the Thirty Years' War (1618—1648) staged between the Protestants and the Catholics of the Holy Roman Empire. In 1644 Bavarian troops plundered and burned the city completely. It remained a ghost city for a year. About a year later some 100 refugees returned to their homes and community life again got its start. Count Johann returned to his country to help rebuild the city, but in 1675 the plague killed many of the population. From 1677 to 1721 the country was reigned by Count Georg August Samuel of Nassau who contributed much to the rebuilding of the city. He was instrumental in enforcing a law that all must help in reconstruction. Although harsh in his dictations, he did much to regain the city's splendor.

Taunusstrasse with its steam trolley in 1880

Market Church and Marktplatz in 1870

The country then underwent two wars — the Spanish War from 1701 to 1718 and the Austrian War from 1740 to 1745. In 1744 the residence of the Princes was moved to Wiesbaden's suburb of Biebrich and the governmental offices of Idstein and Usingen were moved to Wiesbaden. In those days Wiesbaden had 2,000 inhabitants. The city was then too small to take care of the visitors, who during the summer sought the beneficial baths. Thus, the city began an expansion program which is continuing today. Now a city of a quarter-of-a-million people, it is enlarging with the construction of many new facilities. Wiesbaden actually became a tourist and spa city at the beginning of the nineteenth century when the State of Nassau was enlarged and the boundaries of the city were extended so that the construction of new buildings could get underway.

By the year 1815. Wiesbaden was already known as a famous European spa city. By 1825 it was one of the best known "cure" cities in the world. The erection of the first Kurhaus was an indication that Wiesbaden was growing and about to become known as a fabulous resort city. The first Kurhaus was built from 1808 to 1810.

Before construction of the Kurhaus, gambling was conducted on a small scale in the various bath houses. Upon its opening, the Kurhaus introduced a spacious casino with roulette tables which still attracts vacationers from throughout the world. Many attend just to watch the evening's proceedings and to place a few small bets, but the elite gamble heavily and often acquire small fortunes at the wheel of chance.

In 1820 there were 5,500 inhabitants in Wiesbaden. Homes were not too close together and gardening was the main occupation. With the growth of the town, more and more people found use for professional talents and the community began to fill in. It is hard to believe the population is now more than 45 times that which it was some 135 years ago.

On April 13, 1840, the city's first railroad station (The Taunus Station) was opened in Wiesbaden. The line operated between Frankfurt (25 miles away) and Wiesbaden and was the first major commercial transportation to the resort city and the third railway in Germany.

In 1875 Wiesbaden got its first steam trolley. The tracks formed an oval through the main part of the city and the entire distance covered about three miles. In 1896 the first electric streetcars were introduced in Wiesbaden.

Wilhelmstrasse in 1890

At the turn of the century the population of the city had reached more than 86,000. Rapid growth of the spa city was very evident and in five years (to 1905) the population had increased to 100,953. Additional municipal facilities attracted many more persons to the expanding industry and construction workers had little trouble finding work.

In 1905 the Kurhaus was torn down because it was too small to accommodate the carriage trade and construction of the new Kurhaus began immediately. It is now one of the best known buildings in Germany.

From 1907 until the beginning of World War I, Wiesbaden's population and industry increased steadily. Following the war were the lean years and in the late 1920's the city again began to feel prosperity. The city held its own through 1940 and was only moderately damaged during World War II.

Now (1955) Wiesbaden is one of the finest cultural and resort cities in Western Germany. Its first class accommodations and recreational facilities make it second to none in the country.

The Andreas Fair in 1837. The annual event is still conducted today

Wiesbaden's
Main Railway Station

Wiesbaden's Hauptbahnhof (Main Railway Station) is one of the city's most famous landmarks.

It is unlike most main stations in Germany's larger cities in that it is situated by itself and is surrounded by few other large buildings. Adjacent to it are several small business establishments and fronting it is Wiesbaden's beautiful Reisinger Park. Today it houses 12 main tracks.

While few commuters utilize it in comparison with New York's Grand Central Station, its service to the tourist trade can well vouch for its necessity.

From a small gauge railroad eventually evolved the modern depot of today which accommodates streamliners and private trains from all over the continent.

Within the main building itself may be found a fine modern lobby, lounge, dining room and one of the better restaurants in the city. One unique feature of the station is its twin round-houses, which makes it one of the largest dead-end rail terminals in the world.

Reisinger Park

One of Wiesbaden's larger and better known parks is the Reisinger Anlage, located directly across from the main railway station. Its broad promenades, sparkling fountains and beautiful blooming flowers make it one of the city's most scenic views in the spring, summer and autumn. During the mild winter its snow-covered expanse of lawns and ice-capped fountains make it a crystal paradise.

Partially destroyed during World War II, today it has been completely restored and the Wiesbaden populace may be seen strolling along its relaxing expanses.

At night, throughout the year, lights play upon its dancing water fountains — turning it into a wondrous spectacle. Its many pools are bounded by flower beds — boasting blooms of every color and description. Modern statuary and a completely new colonnade grace its glory.

If the description of the park seems a little flowery, it should be pardoned, because the park has been the meeting place of many famed artists, poets and musicians.

Situated on one of the city's main thoroughfares, it is one of the most viewed parks in the city. While it does not abound in trees, except at its edges, its pleasing green lawns and colorful foliage render it one of the most picturesque parks in Germany.

The *Rathaus*
(City Hall)

$\mathscr{E}$very community — from the smallest village to the largest metropolis — is justly proud of its city hall. In Germany the city hall is called the "Rathaus" and houses the city's main governmental body.

Wiesbaden's present Rathaus, located at the Marktplatz (market place), was completed in 1887. Wiesbaden's Oberbuergermeister (Lord Mayor), and his staff moved into the new building's 100 spacious rooms upon completion. Construction took three years, starting in 1884.

Today it houses such offices as the city finance office, tax office, marriage license bureau and, of course, the Lord Mayor's office.

During World War II the building was two-thirds destroyed. It was completely restored in 1950—51.

The basement of the Rathaus is the site of Wiesbaden's Ratskeller, a locally famous restaurant.

The Old Town Hall

The Alte Rathaus (Old City Hall) still stands on Marktplatz Square diagonally across the street from the present-day Rathaus which you have just read about. It is one of the oldest buildings still standing in the history of 2,000-year-old Wiesbaden.

The site of the Altes Rathaus was donated to the city by Count Ludwig in 1608 and two years later the building was opened to the public as Wiesbaden's City Hall.

During the period of the Thirty Years' War (1618—1648) the Rathaus became the center of attacks by hordes of invading troops. Though not destroyed, the building was badly defaced and required much rebuilding and renovation. However, the building retained its present-day outline and foundation.

In the late nineteenth century the building was abandoned and its offices moved to the present Rathaus across the way.

Today the building serves Wiesbaden publically, acting as a utilities building where the gas, water and electric records are kept and bills are paid.

One of Wiesbaden's most attractive landmarks, the Kurpark or Kurgarden, is located behind the fabulous Kurhaus which you will read about later. Tourists, as well as local Wiesbadeners, enjoy its beautiful scenery.

The lake within the Kurgarden is a place for relaxing boating beneath the towering trees as the graceful swans swim contentedly by. A special section of the Kurgarden is known as "Little Nice" and displays an outstanding panorama of exotic plants and colorful flowers. During the summer months, the city of Wiesbaden sponsors many activities in the Kurgarden, such as band concerts and outdoor dances. The city often presents outstanding firework displays and special park illuminations made possible by some 30,000 lights.

The Kurpark

The Old Roman Wall

From the historian's viewpoint — probably one of the most important sites in Wiesbaden is the Old Roman Wall. The beautifully constructed fortification remains today in essentially the same form that it did centuries ago. About 375 A. D. the Romans built a strong wall of defense around Wiesbaden against the marauding tribes of the Alemannen (Germanic tribes). The wall began on the central hill and stretched to the present market place.

A portion of the Old Roman Wall may still be seen on Coulinstrasse giving an aura of timelessness to Wiesbaden.

The Wall was built by the Roman Legions which advanced on Wiesbaden and remained for several centuries. It was these conquerors who believed in the benefits of mineral baths and who established the city as a health resort.

The Neroberg Temple

The temple pictured below is more than 100 years old. Known to the Wiesbaden populace as the Neroberg Temple, it majestically overlooks the famous old spa city.

Gazing from the temple, one may see the sloping Neroberg vineyards which were originally planted during the sixteenth century.

Erected in 1851, the Temple was built as a scenic structure. On clear days one may view the Rhein River Valley to the old city of Mainz and the Main River, as well as the city of Wiesbaden. The roof of the Temple is supported by nine heavy columns which were moved from Wiesbaden's Wilhelmstrasse in the middle of the nineteenth century. They formerly served as lantern posts, equipped with hanging oil-burning lamps.

The Ring Church

The Ring Church (Ring-Kirche) was built in 1892-94 by Professor Otzen of Berlin and is a Protestant Church. It derives its name because of its location on the Kaiser Friedrich and Bismarck Rings at the west end of Rheinstrasse.

The church was constructed in Romanic architecture and established a new era in church-construction style. Position of the interior fixtures deviated greatly from that of churches of the time.

*S*ituated on the northern side of the present-day market place is the graceful, red-stone Markt Kirche. It was under construction from 1853 to 1862. A Protestant Church, its spires are the highest of any church in the city.

The land on which the five-towered house of worship stands today was donated by the Duke of Nassau, Adolf. The designer of the church was Karl Boos, the Duke's personal architect. Of late Gothic style, the cathedral is a must for camera fans.

The Market Church

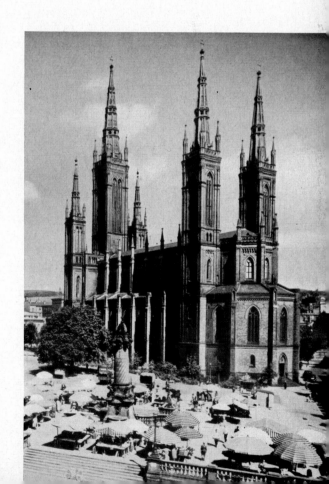

St. Boniface Church

The Church of St. Bonifatius was erected more than 100 years ago. Its cornerstone was laid June 5, 1845, the feast day of its patron Saint. Wiesbaden's foremost Catholic Church, it is located on Luisenplatz.

The Church was named for the first Catholic missionary who came to teach and preach in Germany. Born in England in 680 A. D., St. Boniface spent the better part of his life spreading the story of Christianity to the German people. In 755 A. D. the Saint met death at the hands of barbarians in defense of his faith.

ST. NIKOLAS CHURCH

St. Nikolas Church in Bierstadt, a suburb of Wiesbaden, is not only Wiesbaden's oldest Church, but one of the oldest in Germany. Built during the ninth century, the church was Catholic until the Thirty Years' War from 1618 to 1648. From then until the present time it has been a Protestant Church.

The lower walls of the church and the sealed entrance on the southside (which is adorned by old Christian ornaments) are remains of the old structure.

In the interior of the church may be found figures from the old Gothic pulpit, the Holy Madonna, the Holy St. Nikolas and the Holy Ferrutius. The old altar, formed of 8 paintings, is located above today's altar.

THE RUSSIA

RTHODOX CHURCH

The Russian Orthodox Church is located near the Neroberg Temple. It was built by Duke Adolph of Nassau in memory of his young wife, a Russian princess, who died a year after their marriage. In 1844 the Duke married 19-year-old Elizabeth Michailowna, niece of the Russian Czars Alexander I and Nicholas I. After her untimely death a year later, the Duke began construction of the church on Neroberg Mountain which was part of the property he owned until his death in 1905.

The church was designed after the churches of Petersburg, Russia, by the Duke's personal contractor.

Completed in 1855, the church also serves as a tomb for the beautiful princess.

The church altar is constructed mostly of inlaid gold and sparkles brightly when reflecting beams of sunlight filters through the expensive stained-glass windows.

The five gold-plated towers are symbolic of the Lord Jesus and the four Disciples, Matthew, Mark, Luke and John.

Services are conducted regularly every Saturday and Sunday and on all religious holidays.

Wiesbaden's

Castle

Castles are usually associated with mountain tops and strategic locations for the protection of the occupants. This is not necessarily so, since many were constructed for their beauty and a place of domicile only.

Wiesbaden's Schloss (castle), former residence of Kaiser Wilhelm II, was erected more than 100 years ago. It is located at the market place, forming a triangle with the old and new Rathauses which are featured earlier in this book.

This is not the first castle which was constructed in the city, but is the only one in Wiesbaden proper which stands today.

During the sixteenth century Count Ludwig constructed the so-called "new castle" which formerly was located between the castle's present site and the Market Church. The old castle was removed to make room for today's castle.

Sonnenberg Castle

The old Sonnenberg Castle was built about 1200 A. D. by two counts of Nassau, brothers Heinrich II and Ruppert IV. Sonnenberg is a small community located on the northeastern outskirts of Wiesbaden.

The village did not exist when the castle was built for the Counts of Nassau. Sonnenberg was recognized as a village in 1351.

The castle was plundered during the Thirty Years' War by invading soldiers. Later, inhabitants of the area pilfered stone from the castle walls to make homes for themselves in the valley.

The points of interest of the castle include a dungeon, a castle chapel, 12-foot thick walls, observation towers and open fireplaces.

A locally-famous restaurant is now situated at the site of the old castle. Delicious meals, served with the finest wines of the area, are available here.

Frauenstein Castle

One of the smallest, and one of the oldest, is the Castle Frauenstein, located about five miles from Wiesbaden city proper. Its actual historical name was once "Castle Vrowensteyn".

There is no exact historical date when the castle was built (between the eleventh and twelfth centuries) by the former Dukes of Frauenstein.

Historical documents about the castle have been found only as far back as the thirteenth century. All that remains of the castle today is a square tower and several protection walls. The tower itself includes small square rooms with round stair cases. The knights who once lived within the castle's walls built it on a granite base and part of the east side was added later.

During the middle ages a lake was located near the castle. It was then restrained by dams, and whenever war broke out between neighboring Counts and Dukes, the dams were opened to let the water fill a moat which gave the castle added protection.

Historical documents indicate that the castle maintained its stateliness until 1723. However, around 1803 the local populace began to salvage stone broken loose from its base for house construction. Local government officials soon put a halt to this and today the castle is under governmental control.

Standing majestically on the banks of the famous Rhein River is one of the most romantic of all Rhein castles. Located in Biebrich, a ten-minute drive from downtown Wiesbaden, the "Biebricher Schloss" guards the street which bears its name.

One of the outstanding features of the castle in the late nineteenth century was its splendid gardens and park which covered two square city blocks. The once carefully landscaped and flowered-decked gardens are now used as a public park. Here, every year in May, is held an outstanding international horse and riding show.

Biebrich Castle

$\mathbf{O}$riginating as one of the "pet projects" of Kaiser Wilhelm II, the luxuriously furnished and famous Wiesbaden Opera House has attracted thousands of continental personalities to its significant performances.

Built in Renaissance style, it contains 1,330 seats and occupies an entire square block on Wilhelmstrasse, Wiesbaden's main street. Construction of the building required

The Opera House

only two years and was completed in 1894 at a cost of more than two million Reichsmarks.

In 1923 fire destroyed the stage, which was subsequently rebuilt with modern equipment such as hydraulic lifts, advanced sound effects, lighting and other innovations.

Specially constructed fireproof vaults in the basement of the Opera House contain some 8,000 costumes comprising the most complete operatic wardrobe in Germany. Costumes from this wardrobe can outfit almost every known operatic role.

Famous opera stars from throughout the world have performed on the stage of the fabulous Wiesbaden Opera House.

GOETHE

Johann Wolfgang von Goethe, Germany's foremost philosopher, poet, playwright, novelist and scientist was born in Frankfurt at high noon, August 28, 1749, to the wife of a Frankfurt Imperial Councilor. His statue graces the entrance of the new museum.

The most famous of the author's works, "Faust", was not completed until shortly before his death. Goethe died in Weimar in 1832 at the age of 83.

FRIEDRICH VON SCHILLER

The figure standing in front of the Opera House is Friedrich von Schiller, German poet, dramatist, historian and philosophical thinker. He was born in Marbach of Schwabia in 1759 of poor parents who wanted their son to enter the priesthood of the Lutheran Church.

Among his many famous works are "The Robbers", which won wide acclaim; "Cabal and Love", "Maid of Orleans", and "Mary Stuart"; the last a particular success on the stage. Schiller died May 9, 1805.

Without the person whose statue appears here, Johannes Gutenberg, the printing of this book may have been delayed by several hundred years. Known to millions as the father of the printing press and "movable type", Gutenberg made the first major steps in printing in the new world.

Born in 1397 in the city of Mainz across the Rhein River from Wiesbaden, Gutenberg realized the vast possibilities of a rapid means of reproducing printed material.

The masterpiece of Gutenberg's press was the Mazarin Bible, the earliest book printed in Europe from movable type. The Bible is probably better known to Americans as the Gutenberg Bible. It got its name Mazarin, because the first copy to recapture attention was found in the library of Cardinal Mazarin in Paris. It is sometimes called the 42-line Bible.

The Holy Book required several years to produce and was completed in 1455. Its text is in Latin and the type is a Gothic style related to old English and similar to the best handwriting of the times.

In its design and workmanship, the Mazarin Bible holds its place as one of the finest of all books ever printed. A statue of the famed printer is located on the steps of the Nassauische Landesbibliothek (State Library) on Rheinstrasse.

JOHANNES GUTENBERG

Richard Wagner's Home

This old mansion rests on the banks of the Rhein River at 2 Rheingaustrasse in downtown Biebrich, a Wiesbaden suburb. It was built in 1860 and was made famous by one of the most illustrious of all German composers.

Richard Wagner, who was little-known at the time, rented two rooms on the second floor of the building two years after its completion.

While in Biebrich, Wagner was busy composing his most famous opera, "The Meistersinger". According to some of his letters to friends and loved ones, Wagner started the masterpiece on March 13, 1862. Strolling along the Rhein and taking boat rides gave the young composer inspiration to write the "Meistersinger" and many more of his famous operas.

Today, the only indication that the background of this old mansion on the Rhein is any different from other Biebrich houses is a six-foot redbrick wall where a metal plaque reads: "Here once stayed Richard Wagner, who in 1862 wrote his opera, The Meistersinger".

Thus did a music-loving Germany pay tribute to one of its greatest composers, Richard Wagner — little-known in life, immortal in death.

These people are about to enter the Opera House proper from the foyer on one of its finest evenings — the opening night of the International May Festival. On this occasion, the elite of Wiesbaden and surrounding communities don their best and attend the Opera. The opening of the May Festival is generally considered to be the official coming of spring by local Wiesbadeners. The world-famous festival lasts for four weeks.

Opening Night at the Opera House

The New Museum

One of the largest buildings in Wiesbaden is the new museum. Although it was constructed over 40 years ago, it is still referred to as the new museum since it moved from the old site two blocks away.

Located on the corner of Friedrich-Ebert-Strasse and Wilhelmstrasse, it replaced the 100-year old former museum which still stands on Wilhelmstrasse and houses official government offices.

The museum's 130 rooms are sectioned into three separate divisions; a history museum, a natural science museum, and an art gallery. All are open to the public. Here may be found an exceptional collection of ancient and medieval historical displays and works of art. The history museum offers a vast treasure of German and Roman relics and art pieces. The natural science museum features a zoological department containing one of the largest collections of mounted insects in the world. Almost every species is shown.

The art gallery is mostly devoted to the paintings of contemporary artists. A statue of Johann Wolfgang von Goethe, the great German poet, guards the entrance to the museum.

This majestic structure — a tower of the type often pictured in fairy tales — overlooks the Wiesbaden Golf Course and the valley which leads to Wiesbaden. One of the highest points in the immediate vicinity of Wiesbaden, on a clear day one may see for many miles through the beautiful Taunus Mountains to the Rhein River and the city of Wiesbaden.

The tower's actual name is the Kaiser Wilhelm Tower, but to local Wiesbadeners it is known as Schlaeferskopf (Sleepy-head), since that is the name of the mountain it towers above.

Appearing older than it is, the tower was erected in 1905 by members and friends of the Wiesbaden

SCHLAEFERSKOPF
(KAISER WILHELM TOWER)

Natural Preservation Organization and named after the former German Emperor, Kaiser Wilhelm II, who often hunted on the mountain. The tower's single purpose is, and has been for many years, to offer a kaleidoscopic view of the Rheingau from Mainz to Ruedesheim and the surrounding territory.

Rising almost 100 feet above the top of the mountain which is 1,400 feet above sea level, it was constructed completely of stone found on the mountain.

Fronting the fabulous Wiesbaden Opera House, along with its famous Spielbank (since moved to the Kurhaus) and the Kleines Haus Theater, is the Opera House Colonnade.

The block-long promenade behind the majestic columns presents a panorama of elegant shop windows which display merchandise of the highest quality.

Patrons may find the finest in jewels, furs and other outstanding products exhibited in these showcases. With its modern shops, it is hard to believe that this colonnade was originally built in 1839.

The Opera Hous

Colonnade

Wiesbaden's "Brunnenkolonnade" (Fountain Colonnade) is located across a small park directly opposite the Opera House Colonnade.

The structure was erected in 1826-1827 as a bazaar with the southern extension completely open. The colonnade at that time was a mecca for tourists and foreign travelers.

The colonnade was destroyed during World War II and reconstruction began in 1950. Today it is one of the most beautiful and modern structures in Wiesbaden.

The Brunnen Colonnade

Wiesbaden's "main stem", or Fifth Avenue, is Wilhelmstrasse, named after Duke Wilhelm of Nassau. Immortalized in literature by both Noel Coward and Dostojewski, the street is the hub, the center and the pulse beat of Wiesbaden.

When Kaiser Wilhelm II and his court made their headquarters here at the beginning of the May spa season in the early 1900's, Wilhelmstrasse was the scene of floral displays, gaiety and fashionable Sunday promenades.

It was commonplace for a Hindu Maharajah and his entourage to appear on Wilhelmstrasse. Rolls Royces were parked along the curb amid smart automobiles from dozens of countries.

Today, the street still retains its continental flavor with the most fashionable shops and sidewalk cafes lining its broad expanse. It is the main boulevard and the "lifeline" of social life in this famous international city.

In the mild spring and summer evenings, one may sit at sidewalk tables adorned with gay lanterns and listen to a concert, sip Brazilian coffee prepared in American style and nibble at French and Danish pastries while being served by a pretty German waitress.

Wilhelmstrasse

Warmer Damm Park

History has it that at the time when Wiesbaden was a walled-in city, it was surrounded by many lakes. These lakes dried out around 1730 with the exception of two — the so-called "cold" and "warm" lakes. The cold lake was a fisherman's paradise and the warm lake was a collecting point for warm waters from the city's many hot springs. The two lakes were separated by a dam.

"Warmer Damm" actually means warm dam. The entire area, including today's site of the Opera House, was wilderness in those days. Duke Adolph of Nassau bought the territory in 1860. He converted the area into what is now one of the prettiest parks in the city.

The monument of Kaiser Wilhelm I, facing the lake, was sculptured by Professor Johann Schillings of Dresden. It is made of pure Italian marble and stands on a granite base. Wilhelm I was born March 22, 1797 in Berlin and died there March 9, 1888. He spent many enjoyable hours in Wiesbaden.

Today the park is a perfect setting for relaxation and pastime. A fountain presents a towering cascade in the center of the lake, and waterfowl make it a refuge and are often fed by local townspeople.

*The heart of Wiesbaden's downtown shopping district —
Kirchgasse at Mauritiusplatz*

Wiesbaden's "Fifth Avenue" — Wilhelmstrasse looking south

Although it has since moved next door to the colossal Kurhaus, Wiesbaden's Spielbank (Casino) has, and will ever be, a "must" to visitors of the city. While a great number of the patrons are wealthy people wishing to try their luck on the wheel of chance, many attend to watch the proceedings as they sip a cool drink or have a light meal.

Here, the international set from the four corners of the earth congregate at the roulette wheels and Baccara tables. While a sizeable fortune may be amassed with a few choice bets and a bit of luck, most of the patrons are moderate bettors and are satisfied with a few marks winnings — or losses.

Wiesbaden's Casino

Marktplatz (Market Place)

Perhaps the most picturesque and colorful spectacle that visitors to Wiesbaden may encounter is the local Market Place. The Market Place opens daily at 7 am except Sundays and holidays and closes at 2 pm with the exception of Saturday which is the big day. Here farmers and truck gardeners from the outlying communities bring their produce to sell to the cityfolk. They display their wares on open-air benches under vari-colored tents and canopies.

Gracing the Market Place is a large granite monument with figures depicting the four seasons and Gods and Goddesses of the harvest.

The Marktplatz was built in 1901 and the monument was built by the official state architect, Genzmer. The market elevation is set with tile and occasional slabs of glass. The purpose of the glass insets is to give light to the underground storage which is so large that the merchants' tables, stalls and unsold products may be kept there overnight. Adjoining the Market Place is a flower place. It extends along a narrow "traffic island" for nearly a full city block. Here may be found flowers of every variety that are in season.

Throughout the year, produce of every description may be purchased at the Market Place. Business naturally slows down during the cold weather, but during the summer one may buy anything from strawberries to mushrooms, turnips to oranges, or poultry to gardenias.

The Fabulous Kurhaus

Undoubtedly the most photographed and certainly the most famous structure in Wiesbaden is the Kurhaus. (Kur in German actually means cure, however, it is the center of social life, international exhibitions, and a place of general relaxation.)

The second of two great buildings, today's Kurhaus was erected from 1905-07. The luxury and cosmopolitan splendor of the Kurhaus has always been a magnet that attracts dignitaries and high-ranking persons from throughout the world. Millionaires, kings, diplomats, poets, writers, scientists, artists, musicians and a multitude of other elite make this one of their favorite meeting places to relax in its languid comfort and sip a cognac or quaff a cool beer.

In the right wing of the structure is one of the most fabulous ballrooms in Europe which can accommodate approximately 2,500 people. This newly reconstructed ballroom is the site of the annual carnival ball and other gala celebrations too numerous to mention.

The Fabulous Kurhaus

The Kurhaus restaurant is second to none and features delicious foods of an international variety.

Now housed in the left wing is the Spielbank (Casino) which was discussed earlier in this book and moved to the Kurhaus in November, 1955.

The present Kurhaus was reconstructed, with the exception of the portion known as "column hall", costing over $2,000,000. Hub of cultural activity in this famous city, it is fronted by a block-long park with two beautiful lighted fountains. The Park in olden days was the city bowling green ... Wiesbadeners still refer to it as the "Bowling Green", using the English expression.

*F*uture visitors to Wiesbaden may find this site somewhat hard to locate since it was undergoing an extensive "renovation and face-lifting" at the time this book was published.

However, the exterior of the renowned Kochbrunnen (Boiling Well) matters little, because the waters from the famous well are known for their great healing powers the world over.

Owned and operated by the city of Wiesbaden, the Kochbrunnen Well keeps boiling and bubbling, giving out over 500,000 quarts of the highly mineralized liquid every day. 2,000-year-old Wiesbaden has a deserved fame for these

THE KOCHBRUNNEN

springs. The importance attached to public baths by the Romans is well known. It would seem probable that their first advantage in Wiesbaden was formulated when the news of the existence of thermal springs was brought into their camp at Mainz in the year 10 B. C. One can imagine wealthy Roman ladies dressed in their best white robes, golden sandals, and hand-worked jewelry as they sipped at the Kochbrunnen.

An Architect's Drawing of the new Kochbrunnen

These two towering columns are all that remain of the original Kurhaus. It was constructed in 1810 and was torn down to make way for the new Kurhaus in 1904 - 05. The columns are maintained more or less as a memorial and their style testifies to the majestic splendor that was the first Kurhaus.

In those days, the spacious salons and beautiful colonnades housed exclusive bazaars, gold-framed mirrors, parquet floors, white marble statues and marvelous interior architecture.

The columns now stand adjacent to the present-day Kurhaus in the beautiful Kurgarden.

The Kurgarden

THE FAULBRUNNEN

Centuries ago the Faulbrunnen was known as "Lazy Woman's Well" because the women who frequented the location spent many hours in idle gossip.

The English translation of "Faulbrunnen" is lazy or rotten well. It is called this because, to some, the water from the well has a smell and taste of slightly overaged eggs. However, despite its somewhat disagreeable smell and taste, many persons will vouch for its definite medicinal powers.

Today's Faulbrunnen was drilled in 1842. In those days the city had a hired man in charge of the well's upkeep. In the years that followed, the well changed faces many times. Its present walls were built in 1910 of gray sandstone.

The original source of the Faulbrunnen is located at 9 Faulbrunnenstrasse where the remnants of an old Roman bath house and other Roman treasures were once unearthed.

Doctors and health specialists state that the water from the Faulbrunnen is pure and definitely helps to combat many diseases and human ailments.

Baeckerbrunnen in English means Baker's Well. This quaint Gothic structure is located in a section of town known as old Wiesbaden.

History has it that the well is one of many discovered by the Romans. Today this mineral well satisfies the minds and bodies of many contemporary types. Its natural temperature is approximately 120 degrees Fahrenheit and has a saltwater taste. City mineralogists assert the water contains considerable mineral-salt, crystal, iron and sulphur.

The reason for this well's particular name, "Bakers' Well", is because the bread merchants almost exclusively used the warm salt water in their bread making.

Waters from the well are supposedly beneficial in the curing of stomach, throat and gastric ailments. Bathing in the water is said to help other aches and pains such as rheumatism, arthritis, etc.

Many structures have been built to house the well. It has weathered sieges, time and constant usage. Once privately owned, the "fortunes of war" finally delivered it into the hands of the city government which opened it to the general public.

Kaiser Friedrich Bad

The Kaiser Friedrich Bad, ("Bad" in German means bath) located near the Continental Hotel on Langgasse, attracts visitors from all over the world. The bath house was built between 1910 and 1913 at a cost of about 3,000,000 marks.

A main part of the famous health establishment — the bath — offers many kinds of baths, massages, irradiations, and sun treatments and gets its beneficial waters from the second greatest natural source in Wiesbaden. The Kaiser Friedrich Bath is located in the largest structure that accommodates a bath house in the city. It is especially noted for its thermal baths, and the natural temperature of its waters is 120 degrees Fahrenheit.

Persons suffering from almost every malady known to man have sought relief from its medicinal vapours — many to great satisfaction. It is said to have definite value in helping cases of rheumatism, arthritis and other aches and pains of the body.

The bath is a part of the ancient city which was established by the conquering Romans, shortly after the Birth of Christ. While the building which houses the bath is comparatively new, the soothing waters are the same that brought relief to the Romans and many generations and nationalities since then.

Statue of the Count of Nassau

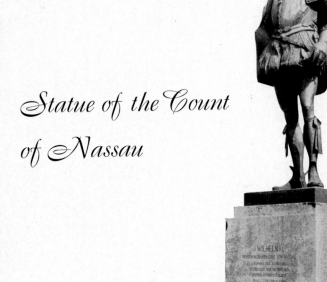

Wilhelm I, Count of Nassau and Prince of Orange, was born in April, 1553. His noble birth entitled him to early tutorage by no less a teacher than Maria, Queen of Hungary and sister of Charles V.

His statue now graces the lawn in front of the five-towered Market Church which stands adjacent to the City Hall. After joining the Emperor's Court, his intelligence and cleverness brought him fame, and he was often consulted on important matters of state. In fact, the Emperor made him commander of the armies at the tender age of 22.

Wilhelm I introduced Christianity to the lands of Holland, Zealand, Utrecht, Gelderland and Friesland, knitting them into a closer union and laying the foundation of the present-day Republic of United Netherlands. He was murdered in 1584 through the plans of a vicious European ruler who sought to break the unity he had established.

The Henkell
Champagne Factory

One of the most interesting tours that may be taken in Wiesbaden is a trip to one of Germany's largest champagne factories, the Henkell wine cellars, located at 142 Biebricher Allee. The tour offers a factual background for the wine connoisseur and many interesting sidelights for the layman.

Founded in 1832 by Adam Henkell, the business of blending and aging champagnes has passed down to the present day through six generations of the Henkell family.

An interesting aspect of this champagne inheritance may be found in the Blue Room, a reception center for private guests on the first floor of the large building. A large stained glass window is inscribed with a poem commemorating the efforts of the various members of the family, set off with colorful city and family emblems.

Under this tremendous building are five wine cellars. They serve various purposes. Some are for the different stages of storage which the finest champagnes must go through and some hold rows of huge wooden casks for the blending process. A network of conveyor belts carries the bottles from one cellar to another. The filling, corking and labeling of the bottles are done by both machines and human hands.

KIRCHGASSE (Church Street)

One of the better known streets in Wiesbaden — both to visitors and the local populace — is Kirchgasse. Considered by many as the "heart" of the city, it runs for almost a mile through the main shopping district. The street itself is actually longer, but in German tradition, it has two names — the other half being known as Langgasse.

Along this byway, shops of every description can be found and goods to try the human imagination may be purchased. Everything is sold — expensive jewelry, Black Forest cuckoo clocks, leather ware, name-brand chinaware, trinkets and knick-knacks. Department stores, clothing stores, cafes, cabarets and theaters are located here.

Pictured above is Marktstrasse in earlier days. Though the tower doesn't exist today, the thoroughfare remains. The fountain in the foreground is still a Wiesbaden landmark.

The tower was 130 feet high and one of four observation towers when Wiesbaden was a walled-in city during the Roman regime. It was called Uhrturm (Clock Tower) because it was the only one of the four towers which had a clock. In those days the second floor was used as a storage room, and a bellringer and his family lived on the top floor. Being a watchman, of course, his main duty was to ring the bell in case of fire or alarm.

The tower itself was torn down in February of 1873, but the old house that was connected with it on the right still remains.

The house itself was called "Zur Muenze" (to the mint) because this is where money was coined in the old days. In 1534 a restaurant took over the site. Until today a restaurant has remained and has been known as the Uhrturm in remembrance of the old tower.

A section of the old town wall may still be found in the cellar of the establishment. Although the building itself has been somewhat modernized, many features of olden times may still be found on a visit to the Uhrturm.

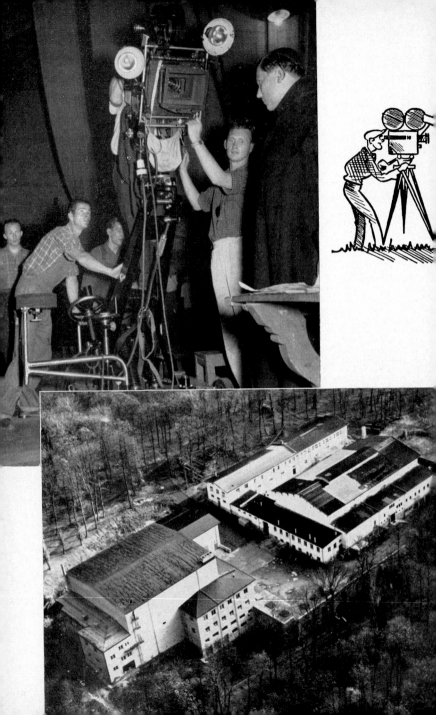

Wiesbaden's Movie Studios

Wiesbaden's film studios are located on the northwestern outskirts of the city and are surrounded by a forest of giant oak and birch trees. Wiesbaden is known as one of the foremost movie producing cities in Germany. The charms of the surrounding countryside are invaluable assets in the filming of outdoor scenes. The Rhein Valley and Taunus Mountains are within easy reach, and the old and fashionable city offers a background which many directors have seen fit to utilize.

The general location in Wiesbaden is easily accessible to performers from the Hessische Staatstheater (State Theater) in Wiesbaden and from the Frankfurt and Mainz stages.

The premises (total area of over 100,000 square yards) house three large indoor studios with a floorspace of more than 2,000 square yards. Studios two and three are newly constructed and fully equipped with the latest production paraphernalia.

Color films, as well as black and white, are photographed by the most up-to-date cameras and photographic apparatus available. Lighting equipment is adaptable to both alternating and direct current.

Of particular importance from a production viewpoint is the modern copying plant. It is a new installation which began operation in October of 1949.

May Festival

The International May Festival of Wiesbaden was held for the first time in 1896, nearly two years after the formal opening of today's Opera House. In those days it was referred to as the Royal Opera House and today is known as the Staatstheater (State Theater).

The idea of the May Festival is credited to Georg von Huelsen, then director of the opera house. The first May Festival took place from May 6-19, 1896. During the two-week celebration, the famous operas of "The Magic Flute", "Preziosa", "Theodora", "Tannhaeuser", "The Flying Dutchman", "The Meistersinger", "Julius Caesar", "Lohengrin" and "Walkuere" were presented.

An outstanding personality at every May Festival from its origin until World War I, was Kaiser Wilhelm II. The festival remained almost obscure until its revival in 1950. Today it has regained its prominence as one of the foremost European operatic spectacles.

The Nerotal Tennis Courts

Boasting some of the finest clay courts of any in the world, the Nerotal Tennis Courts (Nerotal in English means Nero's Valley) are located on the northwestern edge of the city. They may be found about 200 yards beyond the lower station of the Neroberg Cable Trolley (featured earlier). Wiesbaden has two well-known tennis courts, however, the Nerotal Courts are more famous. Here, every year in May, the finest tennis players from throughout the world gather for the International Tennis Tournament.

The oldest courts in the city, the Blumenwiese, are located on Parkstrasse and were too small to accommodate the increasing popularity of the sport which was first brought to Germany by the British.

When Wiesbaden's Tennis and Hockey Club was formed, members met with city officials and construction of the new courts was planned. Nerotal was selected as the best site and building began around 1926. It was necessary to alter the course of a small stream before the courts could be laid out. Wiesbaden's tennis courts, along with those in Bad Homburg and Bad Nauheim, are Germany's finest and oldest.

Construction cost about three-quarters of a million gold Marks and was paid for by the city. There are 14 first-rate courts at the Nerotal. Nearby is a clubhouse for members and guests.

Wiesbaden's Golf Course is located about five miles from the heart of the city to the northwest and is nestled in a scenic little valley in the foothills of the Taunus Mountains. The course which is presently in use is a nine-hole layout and has been in existence since 1912.

Wiesbaden's Golf Club was founded in 1895 and is one of the oldest clubs in Germany. The club's first course was located on the opposite side of town where Wiesbaden's airfield is today. The course is adjacent to a small railway station and community known as Chaussehaus. Money for its construction in 1912 was donated by members of the exclusive club. From 1928 to 1930 the course was enlarged and modernized.

The 2,867-yard links is situated in the valley leading from the base of the Schlaeferskopf (Sleepy Head) Mountain (which has been discussed earlier in this book) to the city of Wiesbaden. A par 35 course, it is well-trapped and has some of the "trickiest" putting greens of any links in Europe. A small stream runs through the center of the course contributing water hazards to four of the nine holes. The stream also borders the edges of fairways on three of the holes.

One of the annual features of the course is the "Henkell Memorial Amateur Tournament" which is usually held in late May and attracts top amateur golfers from all over the continent.

The Hallenbad Indoor Swimming Pool

Wiesbaden's postwar population increase brought about the need for an additional indoor swimming pool, and construction of the beautiful Hallenbad started in the spring of 1952. It was completed in late 1953.

The new pool is located at 144 Mainzerstrasse. The ultramodern pool, based on the latest technical and sanitary research techniques, was converted from a former power plant building.

The Hallenbad actually houses two pools — one for swimmers and the other for non-swimmers and children. Filters and purification plants clear the swimmer's pool three to seven times daily while the children's pool is cleaned as many as 12 times daily, according to attendance.

The pool has two modern chlorination devices. One is a reserve chlorinator and the other is for permanent use. The chlorinator in use is automatically controlled. However, a chemist is available for bacteriological tests and controls.

All temperatures are remotely controlled and constant. Benches surrounding the pool are heated, diving boards range from one to seven-and-a-half yards in height, and a water slide is available for children.

Kleinfeldche

Outdoor

Swimming

Pool

Wiesbaden's newest outdoor swimming pool is called "Kleinfeldchen" by local Wiesbadeners and has been in operation since the summer of 1951. "Kleinfeldchen" translated actually means "Little Field" and derived its name from one of the city's famous soccer fields and handball courts located nearby.

Situated in the western section of this spa city, it has been claimed by many as the finest and most modern in the German Federal Republic.

Located 165 yards off Dotzheimerstrasse, the street leading to one of Wiesbaden's major suburbs, Dotzheim, the pool offers a wonderful view of wood-surrounded Neroberg, the sister outdoor pool "Opelbad", the Neroberg Temple, "Kaiser Wilhelm Tower" and many other points of interest.

About 6,000 persons may enjoy facilities of this super-swimming installation. One large 60 by 170 foot swimming pool is equipped with seven racing lanes for regular swimming and tournaments. Next to it is a special diving pool with diving boards ranging up to 10 meters (about 35 feet) in height. Other attractions include a non-swimmer's pool and a kiddies' pool which were added in 1952.

Numerous dressing rooms are offered. There are also showers and wash rooms as well as a lifeguard station. A restaurant accommodates outdoor terraces, and a 22,000 square-yard area is available to sun bathers.

Photo contributed by the Three Lilies publication, the "Wiesbaden 1956 Picture Calendar."

The Neroberg Vineyards

These special and well-kept vineyards grace the sides of the Neroberg. Looking from the Neroberg Temple one may see the sloping vineyards which were planted during the sixteenth century. The small quantity of exclusive wines produced by the Neroberg vineyards is limited to sale in Wiesbaden.

Soehnlein

Rheingold

The Soehnlein Rheingold Champagne Cellars, located in Schierstein, a Wiesbaden suburb, were founded January 11, 1865. Old files, dating back to that time, state that permission was first given to construct the company by the ducal Nassau Landes Government of Wiesbaden. Two years after the company's foundation, the first champagne was awarded a medal of excellence at the Paris World Exhibition. Nine years later, the excellent wine won a gold medal at the World Exhibition at Philadelphia. One of the most modern factories in Europe, the fine wine cellars produce several million bottles of champagne each year. Every bottle ages at least four years before it is put on the market. This aging requires continual inspection and agitation to produce the light, bubbling wine.

The wine is first stored in giant casks in the initial part of the aging process and then bottled. After being aged in the bottles, the wine is then purified, the bottles corked and sealed and the final wrapping applied.

During important celebrations, such as weddings, anniversaries, birthdays, national holidays and the Carnival season, champagne (or Sekt as it is known to the German people) is the traditional beverage.

This magnificent swimming pool with its spacious lawns has been a popular swimming and sun-bathing locale for Wiesbadeners and visitors for more than 20 years. It is situated majestically overlooking the city of Wiesbaden on the Neroberg (Nero's Mountain).

A ten or fifteen-minute drive from downtown Wiesbaden, the Opelbad was opened to the public June 16, 1934, following two years of construction. It cost a little over 300,000 marks (About $100,000 in those days) and was financed by Wilhelm von Opel, of the Opel Auto-

mobile Company in nearby Ruesselsheim.

The pool has a large filtering and purifying system which completes a changing cycle three times daily and contains some 1,600 cubic meters of water. Initial filling of the pool at the beginning of summer takes 15 days.

Bathers have every modern convenience. The pool facilities include a wading pool for youngsters, a water slide, diving boards, extensive locker facilities, showers, a sun terrace and a small cafe where refreshments may be purchased, plus a badminton and other small games area.

The Opelbad Swimming Pool

The Neroberg Cable Trolley Car

A masterpiece of engineering is the Neroberg Cable Trolley Car which climbs up the steep side of the Neroberg Mountain from the valley near the tennis courts to the site about a half-mile away, overlooking Wiesbaden near the Opelbad swimming pool.

Construction of the small railway was completed September 25, 1888, and operation was taken over in 1925 by the Wiesbaden Transit Co. The cars are equipped with gears which control the speed.

The trolley offers visitors a wonderful view of Wiesbaden as it goes up the hill. It actually was built so that people may visit the Neroberg Temple from which one may see all of Wiesbaden, Mainz across the Rhein River and much of the Rhein Valley on clear days.

In its long and varied history, Wiesbaden tallied among its collection of miscellanea, a real, live Robin Hood — as genuine as any green-shirted sprite who ever lurked in the dark shadows of Sherwood Forest.

Wiesbaden's Raeuberhauptmann" (captain of the robbers) was by name one Heinrich Anton Leichtweiss. At the time of his prowling local premises, from 1781 to 1788, his cave home was a far cry from the historical site it is today. However, it remains one of the more popular visiting points for visitors.

The Robber's Cave

The cave was — in those days — a four-room and loft layout, complete with pantry, fireplace, built-in plumbing and a bulletin board, giving the target for the night.

For seven years the band lived in their remarkable underground headquarters before being betrayed by the smoke from their fireplace. A company of city police dug them out and eventually Heinrich was executed.

Today the cave may be visited and many of its fabulous relics — old weapons and a money vault — are still intact. It is located past the Nerotal Tennis Courts and is known to Wiesbadeners as the "Leichtweiss Hoehle."

FaSchiNg

"Fasching" is to the German people what Mardi Gras is to Americans and the Carnival of Nice is to the French. The celebration starts slowly during the middle of November and reaches its climax during a special three-day period prior to Ash Wednesday.

Actually, there is little proof of the origin of the "fool's festival". History tells of bacchanals in Greece and Rome as well as of heathenish cults and festivals in Germany of long ago. Many customs of these festivals are believed to have been carried over to the present day, although greatly moderated.

Through tradition the festive season has remained and "Fastnacht" (night before Lent) is now limited to three days. The three days — Sunday, Monday and Tuesday before Ash Wednesday — are the main days of celebration for the season. Giant dances and extravagant balls are highlights of the celebration which is touched off with a gala parade in Germany's principal cities. Each city and town elects a Prince and Princess of Carnival to preside over the festivities. Throughout the Fasching period the emphasis is on fun. For three days all inhabitants are subject to the "code of fools" which provides for foolish freedom and a general good time by all.

This incongruous, dirty-faced gentleman who nonchalantly strolls about the streets of Wiesbaden in a battered top-hat, swallowtails or cutaway, is ever a cause of wonderment to visitors of the fair city. He is, in the costume of his trade, a chimney sweep.

Actually, this comical looking mimic of the opera-going set, is more or less regarded as a personage, and known to the Germans as a "Schornsteinfeger." As such, he appears with his ropes, brushes and brooms, in pursuit of one of the oldest and most respected professions since the first European chimney. Traces of his previous visits may be found on the roof-top scoreboards which he keeps.

A popular legend about the chimney sweep is that a few days before he appears to clean a chimney on his regular rounds, he draws the sign of a ladder on the front doorstep of the house. To destroy or obliterate this sign is supposed to bring "bad luck" upon the residents of the house.

All in all, the chimney sweep has proven an unimpeachable man characterized in the legends with which the old world has surrounded him. Cheerful, obliging, and with a smile that shines readily from his work-blackened face, he is a rugged, efficient worker of a proud profession.

The Local Chimney Sweep

Wagemannstrasse

A small obscure alleyway which runs parallel to Kirchgasse about 50 yards away is Wagemannstrasse, a famous and infamous street which extends for about 300 yards between Marktstrasse and Goldgasse. It is one of the oldest streets within the old walled city, once utilized by the ancient Romans.

The street was laid out by the Romans in their heyday as the direct center of the city. It is still in the middle of the downtown district, and runs from the Goldener Brunnen Hotel to the Maldaner Cafe.

Wagemannstrasse was originally called Metzgergasse (Butcher's Alley) because of the great number of meat markets lining its way.

The street is a mecca for hunters of genuine antiques, but it also has more than its share of peddlers of "rare" paintings and "discounted" porcelain.

The street has an atmosphere in a class with London's Limehouse section, New York's Bowery and Paris' Montmartre.

We now journey to another Wiesbaden suburb — the small community of Schierstein. Situated on the banks of the Rhein River, its harbor has been made into a fine water refuge for small craft and is the site of an annual summer festival.

Formerly, Schierstein bordered an exceptionally broad place on the Rhein, with two long islands situated about 500 yards off shore in the middle of the river. The extreme ends of these islands were joined with the mainland to form a large oval with one natural entrance-exit to the Rhein River between the two islands.

On one shore of the harbor opening is the German rescue station and on the other is a private swimming and boating club.

In early days the harbor was used for delivery of wood, coal, sand and gravel. Today its primary use is that of a security station for small craft when the Rhein freezes.

Many sporting facilities are available during the summer months among which are boating, water skiing, swimming and other water sports.

Several private boating and swimming clubs are now located at one end of the harbor and many restaurants are situated along the shores.

Schierstein Harbor

A Rhein River Cruise

A visit to Germany, and especially to Wiesbaden, would not be complete without taking a leisurely boat ride on the celebrated Rhein River. Thousands have enjoyed an afternoon, or perhaps a full-day cruise on this distinguished waterway.

Wiesbaden's main point of embarkation for a full-day excursion on the Rhein is usually at the pier in Biebrich, a nearby suburb. Tours may be taken on a variety of vessels — from steamboats to power launches.

Let us take a mythical trip aboard one of the largest boats — a steamer. We will probably board the craft in mid-morning, at about nine o'clock. On this cruise we will travel northward "down" the Rhein, since most points of interest are in that direction.

The majestic Rhein is one of the few major rivers in the world which flows to the north. Some 700 miles long, this glorious silver ribbon winds its way through Germany and is one of the most important waterways in the world for commerce. It is to Germany what the Mississippi is to the United States.

The Rhein River is born with the melting shows of the Swiss Alps. It takes its river form above the Lake of Constance in Switzerland and continues to the towering falls of Schaffhausen and thence to the city of Basel on the southern German Border. Termed as one of the most beautiful rivers in the world, a trip along the Rhein affords a multitude of picturesque views of fertile fields, lofty mountains, abundant vineyards and stately medieval castles.

The Rhein at Wiesbaden-Biebrich

Once aboard the steamer, one begins an unforgettable journey through a storybook land. The story of the Rheinland is, indeed, the story of old Germany.

The order of the day, after the steamer leaves the dock, is to settle back in a comfortable seat, sip a glass of tasty Rhein wine and let fabulous old Germany go gliding slowly by.

For more than 2,000 years German life has been symbolized by the Rhein River. A world of folklore is established by the remains of fantastic old castles which still grace its banks.

While on this cruise down the Rhein we shall pass many interesting towns and points of prominence. However, we will take in only the most significant of these features.

Hattenheim

This small village is noted for its outstanding wines which are considered by connoisseurs to be some of the finest to come from the vineyards of the Rhein Valley. The old monastery Eberbach overlooks the village and has long been established as one of the strong points of Christianity in Germany. Much of the recent German religious film "Martin Luther" was photographed at the monastery.

Ehrenfels Castle near Ruedesheim

Ruedesheim from the Rhein

Ruedesheim

Wine capital of the Rheingau (Rhein territory) is the city of Ruedesheim. On the east bank of the Rhein, it is the first principal town to be noted after leaving Wiesbaden traveling northward. It is the center of the wine industry of Germany and annually thousands of people journey here to take part in the "Weinfest" (Wine Festival).

Many old wine cellars have been remodeled into cafes and restaurants. Situated underground, they are somewhat dank and damp during the cooler months, but are a welcome relief to the temporate summer humidity.

During the Weinfest, wine "tasters" from all over the continent attend. An amazing fact about the foremost local tasters is that after a sip of unlabeled wine, they are able to determine not only the year the wine was made, but the exact vineyard where the grapes were grown.

Main attraction of the town is Drosselgasse, most famous and one of the narrowest streets. Here are found wine cellars and restaurants which serve the wines that have made the town fascinating.

Watch on the Rhein

One of the largest monuments in Germany is Niederwald Denkmal, known to many as the "Watch on the Rhein." Overlooking Ruedesheim, this huge bronze statue is some 75 feet in height and is Germany's National Monument. The base of the statue is approximately 50 feet square. It was erected between 1877 and 1883.

The statue may be reached either by enclosed chair-lift from the town of Ruedesheim or by driving up the narrow road through the vineyards which surround the statue. It is situated on the Niederwald Mountain, bordering the Rhein Valley, and from this site one may see for 15 to 20 miles along the Rhein, on either side of Ruedesheim.

Near the monument is a fine restaurant where delicious meals are served.

Bingen

One of the principal cities on the west shores of the Rhein between Wiesbaden and Koblenz is Bingen, which guards the entrance of the Nahe River into the Rhein.

Located near Bingen, on an island in the Rhein, is the "Mouse Tower". Legend has it that a wicked Bishop once called all the poor people of the area together in a barn and subsequently burned them to death during a time of famine.

God, to punish the Bishop, sent a plague of mice after him and the Bishop retreated to his island. However, the mice swam the Rhein to the island and devoured the cruel Bishop. The tower still remains and is a constant reminder of the ancient folklore and tales of the fabulous river.

The Lorelei

A "must" to visitors is the site of one of the best-known of all German legends — The Lorelei. An enormous mountain of rock emerges almost vertically out of the river. Without the roadway, which has been cut out of the precipice, it would be a sheer drop of more than 100 yards from the top of the edifice to the swiftly-flowing Rhein below.

Everyone should be familiar with the age-old legend of the golden-voiced maidens who lured unsuspecting sailors to their doom upon the jagged rocks beneath.

At this point on the river is one of the narrowest, yet deepest parts. Here it is only about 170 yards in width and approximately 85 feet in depth.

St. Goar and St. Goarshausen

Continuing our trip down the Rhein, we come to the romantic old towns of St. Goarshausen (on the east bank) and St. Goar (on the west). The two towns are located almost directly opposite each other on the banks of the Rhein.

In olden days, near St. Goarshausen on hills overlooking the town, were two castles and the ruins may still be found today. The foremost was known as "Burg Katz" which leered down at its rival castle, nicknamed "Burg Maus". Translated, they are known as the Cat and the Mouse castles. They received their names because the larger and higher castle loomed over the smaller as though it were a cat ready to pounce upon a mouse. Original name of the big castle was Katzenelnbogen which means cat's elbow.

As with most castles built in the Medievel Ages, these were located on the higher points in the area, both for the strategic value and for the purpose of the castle lords keeping an eye on their workers.

Castle Stolzenfels

Continuing our journey to its final point, Koblenz, we pass the impressive castle of Stolzenfels, "The Proud Rock", and the impregnable Fortress Ehrenbreitstein, the mightiest fortress on the Rhein. These are two of the great castles lurking high above the great river on the rampart cliffs.

During olden days, kings and knights were the usual land owners of these fabulous estates and occupants of the castles. However, there were many robber barons who inhabited some of the structures, and their unfair treatment of their workers and neighbors were the cause of many minor wars and clashes.

Koblenz

One of the major water junctions along the Rhein is the point where the Moselle River joins Germany's "father of waters" at Koblenz. One of the larger cities on the river, Koblenz is famous for its towering cathedral and has the first bridge across the Rhein north of Wiesbaden.

Wines from the banks of the Moselle, one of the Rhein's major tributaries, are said to be second only to those of the Rhein Valley. Many prefer the sweeter wines from the Moselle, and doctors often prescribe them for certain maladies.

The facts and legends of the Rhein are represented by the impressive ruins of old castles, but the great beauty of the Rhein River as it flows between gigantic cliffs and past quaint little villages may be found in the quiet everyday life and neighborliness which is the keynote of the inhabitants.

A journey on the Rhein, through the peaceful vineyards which produce some of the world's finest wines, past the enchanting castles of yesteryear, and through the cradle of German history, should be one of the most enjoyable and memorable that a person may experience.

A typical village on the Rhein